Debtburn

Debtburn

Matthew Petchinsky

1

Debtburn: How to Obliterate What You Owe Forever

By: Matthew Petchinsky

Introduction: The Roots of Debt and the Rise of Debtburn

In the shadowed corners of modern society, debt has become more than a financial inconvenience—it is a silent epidemic, engineered by design and perpetuated by tradition. Today, millions wake up not to the sound of opportunity, but to the dull ache of bills, balances, and the relentless pressure to "make it work" within a system rigged for them to fail. Student loans, credit cards, payday advances, and mortgage chains: these are not mere tools, but links in a web expertly spun to keep the majority trapped, compliant, and perpetually paying.

How did we get here? The story goes deeper than poor spending habits or momentary lapses in judgment. Modern debt traps are the evolution of centuries-old power structures. They thrive on marketing-fueled aspirations, engineered lifestyle inflation, and the illusion of "good debt." Financial institutions, with their glossy advertisements and seemingly helpful advisors, encourage us to borrow for education, cars, holidays, and even basic survival. Meanwhile, the fine print lengthens, interest quietly compounds, and the original promise of financial freedom mutates into a cycle of dependence.

Worse, the advice most people receive—whether from mainstream gurus, government agencies, or well-meaning family—is less a map out than a maze. "Stick to a budget." "Cut out coffee." "Pay the minimums and eventually you'll be free." These mantras, repeated like prayers, may offer comfort, but rarely true relief. They ignore the psychological hooks buried in debt contracts and the relentless grind of a system that profits from your confusion, guilt, and exhaustion.

Traditional personal finance guidance is a polite invitation to play by the rules of the house—rules written by those who own it. The result is decades spent in compromise, anxiety, and resignation, with only fleeting glimpses of progress before the next crisis strikes. In this world, the price of admission is your future, paid in monthly installments.

Debtburn is not for those content to wait and hope. It is a declaration of war on everything that has kept you under the thumb of creditors and false promises.

This book is your weapon. It does not peddle side hustles, empty motivation, or mystical "quick fixes." Instead, Debtburn delivers a ruthless, practical blueprint for total liberation: a system built on brutal financial honesty, renegade strategies that defy conventional wisdom, and psychological rewiring that will smash the shackles of indebted thinking.

Here, you will uncover the origins of your debt—not just the numbers on paper, but the beliefs, habits, and manipulations that brought you here. You will learn how to dismantle every excuse, see through every trick, and ignite a transformation that ends, once and for all, the cycle of owing.

Welcome to Debtburn. The fire starts now.

Chapter 1: The Hidden Cost of Minimum Payments

For most people trapped in debt, the minimum payment is both a lifeline and a leash. It feels manageable, almost merciful—a small number on a statement that says, "You're doing okay. You're keeping up." But this is the first, and perhaps most cunning, illusion of the debt system. Minimum payments are not designed for your freedom. They are engineered for your captivity.

The Origin of the Minimum Payment Trap

To understand why the minimum payment is so dangerous, we need to examine its origin. When consumer credit exploded in the mid-twentieth century, banks and lenders discovered something sinister: by allowing customers to pay just a fraction of what they owed each month, they could keep them indebted far longer—and collect far more in interest—than if they forced timely payoffs. The "minimum payment" became a weapon, cleverly marketed as a helping hand.

A minimum payment, by definition, is the smallest amount a lender will accept to keep your account in good standing. This amount is often calculated as a small percentage of the total balance, sometimes just 1–3%, or even a flat rate plus any accrued interest. To the untrained eye, it looks harmless—affordable, even. But underneath, it is a ticking time bomb.

How Minimum Payments Multiply Your Debt

Let's put this into stark perspective. Imagine you owe $10,000 on a credit card with a 20% interest rate, and your minimum payment is 2% of the balance ($200). If you make only minimum payments, it can take decades to pay off the balance—during which time you might pay two or even three times the original amount in interest. What feels like a manageable monthly obligation becomes an endless treadmill, always moving but never arriving.

This is not an accident. The fine print is designed to maximize lender profits by dragging out your repayment over the longest possible period. Every month, most of your payment covers only the interest—leaving the actual balance barely touched. The longer you take, the more you pay, and the deeper you sink.

The Psychological Toll

Beyond the math, there is a psychological cost. Minimum payments create the illusion of progress, which soothes anxiety and delays real action. You see a small dent in your statement and feel a surge of relief, believing you're moving forward. In reality, you're treading water. This manufactured comfort leads to complacency and, over time, resignation. You accept debt as a fact of life, a "normal" condition of adulthood.

Worse, lenders know this. They depend on it. The system feeds on your willingness to pay "just enough" to keep going, never enough to break free.

The True Cost Over Time

To make the true cost unmistakable, let's revisit the numbers with another example. Suppose you owe $5,000 at 18% interest, and your minimum payment is 2.5% of the balance (about $125 at first). If you make only minimum payments, you'll be paying for over 21 years, shelling out over $8,000 in interest—more than your original debt. If you use that credit card while paying it off, the timeline stretches further, the costs spiral, and the cycle never ends.

Multiply this across multiple accounts—student loans, car loans, personal loans, store cards—and the future you're buying is not one of prosperity, but perpetual obligation.

Who Really Benefits?

Ask yourself: who profits when you pay the minimum? Lenders do—banks, credit card companies, student loan servicers. Every month you remain in debt, they collect interest. The longer you stay, the richer they get. In this sense, minimum payments are not a service, but a product—a slow-drip IV of your hard-earned money into their bottom line.

Breaking the Spell

The first act of Debtburn is to see minimum payments for what they are: a leash, not a ladder. They are the reason so many people "do everything right" and never escape. It is not your lack of effort, or a personal failing—it is a trap set by a system that profits from your struggle.

To break free, you must refuse the minimum. This means confronting uncomfortable truths about your spending, your habits, and the seductive comfort of "good enough." It means finding the resolve to pay more—sometimes much more—than what's asked, and to rewire your mindset from survival to assault.

In the chapters ahead, you will learn the renegade strategies that tear through this illusion, disrupt the profit machines, and put you—not the lender—back in control.

The Lesson: The longer you play by their rules, the more you lose. Minimum payments are not your friend. They are the system's most potent weapon, disguised as mercy.

In Debtburn, you will learn to recognize every hidden cost, every subtle snare, and set fire to the habits and beliefs that keep you chained. The journey starts here: by rejecting the comfort of the minimum and embracing the discomfort of true change. Only then does the path to freedom open before you.

Chapter 2: Targeted Debt Torpedo Tactics

If the minimum payment trap is the anchor that keeps you chained to your creditors, targeted debt torpedo tactics are the explosives that break those chains for good. In this chapter, we shatter the myth that slow, steady, and "safe" payments are the only way out. Instead, you'll discover a direct, aggressive, and highly focused approach that accelerates your escape from debt—without gimmicks, side hustles, or smoke-and-mirrors financial wizardry.

The Philosophy of Attack: Why Targeted Matters

Most mainstream advice preaches balance—spread your payments around, keep everyone happy, and try to keep your credit score afloat. This is slow poison. The reality: when you spread your resources thin, you achieve nothing quickly. You become a perpetual "juggler," managing debt, not eliminating it.

Targeted debt torpedo tactics demand a radical shift in mindset: you're no longer a passive participant, you're a saboteur inside enemy lines. Your job isn't to play nice with your debts. Your mission is to demolish them—one at a time, with ruthless focus and firepower.

Step One: Inventory and Triage

Brutal Honesty Inventory

Begin with absolute clarity. Gather every debt statement—credit cards, medical bills, student loans, payday advances, car notes, personal loans, back taxes. List each with:

- Creditor's name
- Total balance
- Minimum monthly payment
- Interest rate
- Penalties, fees, or upcoming deadlines

Most people avoid this, clinging to the belief that "what you don't see can't hurt you." In reality, this avoidance is exactly what the system wants: for you to remain confused, scattered, and overwhelmed. This step is non-negotiable. Without a map, there is no escape.

Triage: Identify Your High-Value Targets

Review your inventory with a cold eye. Some debts bleed you faster (high interest), while others carry psychological weight (the one that wakes you at 3 a.m.). Highlight:

- The highest interest rate debts ("debt hemorrhages")
- The smallest balance debts ("quick kills")
- Any debt with urgent penalties or legal consequences ("land-mines")

You now have your list of targets. Prepare to engage.

Step Two: Select Your Torpedo—Snowball vs. Avalanche vs. Debtburn Hybrid

The Debt Snowball:
This classic method says to attack your smallest debt first, regardless of interest rate. The win is psychological—paying off a balance quickly builds confidence and momentum.

The Debt Avalanche:
Here, you target the debt with the highest interest rate. This method minimizes the total amount paid over time, but progress may feel slower.

The Debtburn Hybrid Approach:
Forget rigid formulas—choose the strategy that hits your personal pain points hardest. For many, a blend works best:

- Destroy one or two small "quick kill" debts for instant wins
- Immediately pivot to the highest interest "bleeder" with every available dollar

This approach torpedoes morale-sapping debts fast, then shifts maximum firepower to the source of your biggest financial wounds.

Step Three: Focus Fire—All Resources to One Target

Here's where most people fail: spreading themselves too thin, making "a little progress" on everything, but never enough to see real change. Instead:

- Pay the minimum on every debt *except* your chosen target.
- Funnel *every spare dollar, windfall, refund, side gig payout, or found money* to that target debt. This isn't optional. No "extra" dinners out, no impulse buys, no splurges until the target explodes.
- Celebrate each kill—when one debt is vaporized, move immediately to the next. Do not rest, do not relax, do not "take a break" to reward yourself with more spending.

This is not about austerity forever. This is short-term, scorched earth tactics until you are free.

Step Four: Accelerants—Fueling Your Torpedoes

To supercharge your progress, deploy accelerants:

Negotiation and Restructuring:

Contact creditors to ask for lower interest rates, waived fees, or hardship plans. Many will say yes if you show seriousness and a plan.

Asset Liquidation:

Brutal but effective: sell what you don't truly need. Old electronics, unused subscriptions, extra furniture, even a second car. Every dollar becomes ammunition.

Lifestyle Detox:

Cut every expense you can. This isn't deprivation—it's liberation. Cancel, pause, or downsize any non-essential service or habit, at least while you're in "attack mode."

Redirect Windfalls:

Tax refunds, bonuses, cash gifts—every penny goes to the target. "Fun money" can wait until you've secured your freedom.

Step Five: Psychological Warfare—Stay Ruthless, Stay Focused

Creditors count on your fatigue and distractions. They design statements and websites to nudge you into "minimum mode" and complacency. Break the cycle:

- Post your inventory in a place you see daily
- Track your progress with a visible, physical chart—watch the numbers fall
- Celebrate milestones, not with spending, but with rituals that reinforce your commitment (a night walk, sharing your win with a trusted friend, marking a calendar)
- Expect setbacks and fight through them. If an emergency knocks you off course, regroup and resume the assault—never return to minimums as your new normal

What to Expect: The Pain and the Breakthrough

This approach is intense, sometimes uncomfortable. You may feel resentment, guilt, or even shame. That's proof you're breaking out of the system's psychological traps. Most people never get this far.

But when you land your first torpedo—obliterating a debt entirely—the surge of power, control, and clarity is electric. Suddenly, the system loses its grip. You are no longer prey, but predator.

Conclusion: Make Your First Strike Now

Right now, review your inventory and choose your target. Whether it's the smallest debt or the most expensive, the point is to take decisive, focused action. This is not theory—it's war. Every torpedo you fire is a blow against the lie that you must remain forever in debt.

From this moment forward, you're done playing defense. This is the beginning of your financial liberation—one debt at a time, one torpedo at a time. And when you run out of targets, you'll look back and realize: the battle is won, and you are free.

Chapter 3: Financial Fasting: Resetting the Addiction to Spending

To obliterate your debt for good, you must confront a hard truth: most debt isn't just a numbers game—it's a deeply wired habit. In the same way that unhealthy eating is often more about psychology than nutrition, the cycle of overspending and debt is rarely about math alone. To break free, you must reset your relationship with money at the most fundamental level. This is where financial fasting becomes your most powerful tool.

The Psychology of Spending Addiction

Debt thrives on one primary fuel: habitual, unconscious spending. Advertisers, retailers, and even your own brain conspire to keep you in a constant state of want. Every notification, flash sale, loyalty reward, and "limited time offer" is engineered to bypass your logic and trigger impulse. Over time, spending transforms from a conscious choice to a compulsive reflex—one that temporarily soothes boredom, stress, loneliness, or even celebration.

This is not an accident. Neurologically, every purchase releases a surge of dopamine—a "reward chemical" that feels good in the moment, but fades quickly, leaving you seeking the next hit. The pattern is identical to substance addiction: anticipation, consumption, and regret, followed by renewed cravings. The debt industry is acutely aware of this and builds its profits on your inability to break the cycle.

What Is Financial Fasting?

Financial fasting is the deliberate, short-term practice of spending nothing beyond what is absolutely necessary for survival. Like a nutritional fast, it is a cleanse for your mind, habits, and wallet. It forces you to confront the urges, triggers, and false "needs" that drive unconscious consumption. In the crucible of forced restraint, your true financial priorities—and your deepest psychological hooks—are exposed.

But this isn't about deprivation or self-punishment. The purpose is to *reset* your system, break the compulsive loop, and reawaken your power of choice. By removing all non-essential spending, you gain clarity, control, and momentum—crucial ingredients for sustaining your escape from debt.

The Rules of the Fast: Brutal Clarity

There is no "one size fits all," but a true financial fast follows these uncompromising rules:

1. **No Non-Essential Spending.**
   Buy only what you *need* to survive: food, rent/mortgage, utilities, medicine, transportation for work or absolute necessity. That's it.
2. **Cut Out Every "Treat."**
   No coffee runs, takeout, streaming subscriptions, clothes, gadgets, books, apps, games, décor, or upgrades. No Amazon "just browsing." No "I deserve this" loopholes.
3. **Cash Only (If Possible).**
   Leave credit and debit cards at home. Use cash for purchases. The physical act of handing over money makes the reality of spending visceral.
4. **Track Every Cent.**
   Keep a written log (not just an app) of everything you spend. Record the date, amount, and purpose. Awareness is the first antidote to unconscious spending.
5. **Set a Firm Time Frame.**
   Most financial fasts last 7–30 days. Choose a period that feels challenging but achievable. Announce your intention to someone who will hold you accountable.

What to Expect: Withdrawal and Awakening

Stage 1: Discomfort

In the first few days, you will feel restless, irritable, maybe even panicked. Triggers will pop up everywhere—a friend's invitation, a targeted ad, an old habit after a long day. Notice the emotions: anxiety, boredom, frustration, a craving for comfort. *Do not* interpret this as failure. This is the detox. Your brain is recalibrating its reward pathways, and this discomfort is proof you're disrupting a long-held addiction.

Stage 2: Awareness

By the end of the first week, you will notice the sheer *volume* of your spending triggers. You may be shocked by how often you reach for your phone, browse online stores, or rationalize a small purchase. With each urge denied, your awareness sharpens. You start to separate true needs from invented wants.

Stage 3: Empowerment

Once the initial discomfort fades, something remarkable happens: you feel lighter, clearer, and in control. The siren song of consumerism grows fainter. You find satisfaction in using what you already own, in meals cooked at home, in walks instead of outings, in presence rather than purchase. You realize how much of your spending was driven by habit, not happiness.

Stage 4: Redirection

With every dollar saved, you reclaim financial firepower. Redirect these savings directly to your "debt torpedo" target. This rapid progress creates a positive feedback loop—every sacrifice translates to visible, measurable freedom.

Practical Tactics for a Successful Fast

Prepare Your Environment:

Remove temptations: unsubscribe from marketing emails, delete shopping apps, unfollow influencers who trigger spending, and put digital barriers in place (website blockers, calendar reminders of your fast).

Enlist Allies:

Tell a trusted friend, partner, or group what you're doing. Public commitment increases accountability and makes relapse less likely.

Replace Triggers:

When you feel the urge to spend, have alternative rituals ready: drink a glass of water, go for a walk, journal, call a friend, or work on a personal project. Swap consumption for creation or connection.

Reflect Daily:

Keep a "fasting journal." Each night, write down moments you were tempted, how you handled them, and what you learned. Over time, patterns will emerge, giving you powerful insights into your habits.

Plan for Emergencies:

Have a small buffer for true emergencies, but define clearly what constitutes an "emergency" before you begin. Not every inconvenience is a crisis.

The Deeper Reset: Rewiring Your Money Mindset

The ultimate goal of financial fasting isn't just saving money—it's transformation. By depriving your brain of easy rewards, you force it to recalibrate what it values. You rediscover the difference between "enough" and "more." This reset is essential for life after debt: without it, you risk falling back into old patterns the moment your balances hit zero.

You will also realize that so much of modern life is engineered to make you feel incomplete, anxious, or left behind—unless you spend. Financial fasting reveals this for the lie it is. In its place, you build a new core of resilience, gratitude, and self-mastery.

Life After the Fast: New Habits, New Freedom

When your fast ends, you will have a fresh perspective. The cravings will have faded, replaced by discernment. You will think twice before every purchase, asking not "can I afford it?" but "does this move me closer to freedom?"

This is the crucible from which true financial liberation is forged. Without it, every strategy, every payment plan, and every "tip" is just a patch on a sinking ship. With it, you are unshackled—not just from debt, but from the endless cycle of want.

Conclusion: Embrace the Fire, Embrace the Fast

The system is counting on your passivity, your addiction to comfort, and your reluctance to face the hard work of change. By embracing financial fasting, you prove—first to yourself, then to everyone else—that you are stronger than your impulses and braver than your cravings.

This is not a punishment. It is a purification. Step into the fire of discipline, and watch your old habits burn away. On the other side waits not just a zero balance, but a new life—one built on power, purpose, and freedom you never thought possible.

Chapter 4: Slaying the Income Ceiling

One of the most persistent myths in the world of personal finance is that debt is simply a result of spending too much, not earning enough, or failing to follow a rigid budget. This is a lie that keeps millions trapped, scrambling to rearrange the same meager dollars month after month. The deeper truth: for many, debt survives—and even thrives—because of an invisible force few dare to name: the income ceiling.

The "income ceiling" is the unspoken, psychological, and often institutional limit placed on what you believe you can earn. It is the sum of social programming, self-doubt, and external obstacles that conspire to convince you that your earning potential is capped. Most people's financial plans, even their dreams, are built within these artificial boundaries. This chapter will teach you to find that ceiling, smash it to pieces, and liberate yourself from its grip—forever.

The Anatomy of the Income Ceiling

The income ceiling is rarely visible at first glance. It is hidden in phrases like:

- "People like me don't make that much."
- "My boss decides my raise, not me."
- "I don't have any special skills."
- "This is just how things are for people in my industry."
- "Making more is risky, greedy, or selfish."

These beliefs are often inherited from family, teachers, friends, and the very media that shapes our worldview. Over time, they calcify into an inner narrative so powerful that even opportunities sitting right in front of you go unnoticed or unclaimed.

It's not just mindset. Institutions reinforce this ceiling. Employers offer "cost-of-living" raises that barely keep pace with inflation. Job descriptions set salary ranges based on averages, not your true value. Even the gig economy, which promises "unlimited earning potential," quietly suppresses income through algorithms and market oversaturation.

The result? Most people work harder and harder, only to hit a plateau. The harder you grind, the more it feels like you're running in place—because you are.

Step One: Identify Your Personal Ceiling

Begin by confronting your internal beliefs. Take an inventory:

- What do you believe is "the most" you can make in a month, a year?
- When was the last time you seriously considered doubling (or tripling) your income?
- Do you dismiss high-income opportunities as "not for you," "too risky," or "too hard" before examining them?
- Do you immediately look for reasons not to apply for a higher-paying job, start a side project, or negotiate a raise?

Write down your answers, and you will see your ceiling in black and white.

Next, look for external reinforcement:

- Does your employer cap raises or promotions by time, not merit?
- Are your skills or roles undervalued compared to market rates?
- Have you been told "you're lucky to have a job," or that "nobody else is hiring"?

Understanding these forces helps you pinpoint the boundaries that need to be shattered.

Step Two: Smash the Ceiling—Psychological and Practical Breakthroughs

A. Psychological Breakthroughs

The first enemy is your own programming. You must become a ruthless editor of your beliefs:

- **Challenge Every Limitation.**
  Whenever you hear your inner voice say "I can't," "I'm not qualified," or "That's not for me," write it down. Then, for each, ask: *Is this fact or fear? Who benefits from me believing this?* The answers are rarely logical, but emotionally potent.
- **Study Outliers.**
  Read stories of people in your situation who shattered their own ceilings. The internet is full of them—teachers who became consultants, retail workers who became entrepreneurs, hourly employees who built six-figure businesses online. Exposure to possibility creates permission to act.
- **Refuse the Guilt.**
  Society often shames those who want more as "greedy." Remember: wanting more is not about greed—it's about reclaiming agency over your future and refusing to subsidize systems that profit from your limitations.

B. Practical Breakthroughs

Psychology is only the first front. Practical action turns belief into reality:

- **Skill Audit and Repositioning.**
  Inventory every skill you have—even those outside your job description. Can you teach, organize, fix, create, write, persuade, or design? Many people underprice themselves because they focus only on "official" credentials, not the real value they offer.
- **Value Leveraging.**
  Take what you do best and repackage it for higher demand or higher paying markets. If you're a teacher, offer tutoring or curriculum design online. If you're in retail, leverage your customer service skills into virtual assistant roles, remote sales, or support for startups. If you write, code, or design, the world is your marketplace—remote work has demolished geographic limits.
- **Negotiation and Advocacy.**
  Stop waiting for someone else to offer you more. Prepare a case for your next raise, promotion, or freelance rate. Practice your pitch. Document your results. If your current employer won't budge, shop your skills elsewhere. Loyalty to a company that caps your potential is misplaced.
- **Reject Time-for-Money Traps.**
  Find income sources that grow independently of your hours. This doesn't mean falling for "passive income" scams, but building products, writing, or selling services with the capacity to scale. Start small, but start now.
- **Monetize Knowledge and Network.**
  What do you know that others don't? What connections can you leverage? In today's economy, information and access are currency. Host webinars, write guides, teach online, or facilitate introductions for a fee.

Step Three: Overcoming Institutional and Systemic Barriers

Even as you grow, some ceilings are enforced by policies, prejudice, or structural barriers. These are real—but not always immovable.

- **Side-Step the Gatekeepers.**
  If you can't break through where you are, go around. The digital world is a backdoor into almost every industry. Freelancing, self-publishing, e-commerce, and content creation have no gatekeepers. You decide what you're worth.
- **Form Alliances.**
  Network with others who have broken similar ceilings. Share information, resources, and encouragement. "Who you know" has never been more important. Let go of the belief that you must do it alone.
- **Stay Relentless.**
  The system will push back—through skepticism, rejection, or even hostility. Let every "no" strengthen your resolve to find a "yes" elsewhere. You owe your loyalty to your own financial liberation, not to anyone else's comfort.

Step Four: Build Multiple Pathways, Not Just One

Slaying your income ceiling is not a single act, but a campaign:

- **Diversify Your Streams.**
  Never again rely on a single source. Multiple income streams—no matter how small at first—build resilience and possibility. This could be freelance work, digital products, consulting, teaching, reselling, or investment dividends.
- **Automate and Delegate.**
  As your streams grow, automate the routine and outsource the rest. Free your time for new opportunities, higher-value tasks, and creative work.
- **Track and Celebrate Growth.**
  Set bold, specific income targets and track your progress monthly. Celebrate every new milestone, no matter how small. Progress is proof that the ceiling is already cracking.

Step Five: Direct All Growth Toward Freedom

As your income rises, the temptation will be to inflate your lifestyle—this is another trap. Instead, funnel every dollar of new income toward vaporizing debt, building savings, and investing in assets that grow. The time for splurging is *after* you've won your freedom, not before.

Remember: every extra dollar is a weapon against the old system.

Conclusion: From Prisoner to Predator

The income ceiling is real—but it is not indestructible. It is a cage built from fear, habit, and outdated beliefs. By ruthlessly interrogating your own story, leveraging every skill and opportunity, sidestepping gatekeepers, and redirecting new income to your freedom fund, you transform from a prisoner of circumstance into the architect of your future.

The system wants you small, quiet, and compliant. But you are done playing by those rules. Slay your ceiling, claim your power, and let your income become the jet fuel that burns your debts to ash. The world is not limited. Neither are you.

Chapter 5: Becoming Unbankable—In a Good Way

To truly obliterate your debt and achieve total financial liberation, you must take your transformation one step further than the mainstream ever recommends: by deliberately becoming "unbankable." But not in the way the system fears. Instead, you'll redefine the term, stripping away dependence on banks, lenders, and the shadowy infrastructure that profits from your participation. You'll become unbankable not because you are excluded, but because you have made their products, services, and traps obsolete in your life.

What Does "Unbankable" Mean?

Traditionally, "unbankable" is a label slapped on those deemed too risky, unprofitable, or unpredictable for mainstream financial institutions—people without steady jobs, credit scores, or conventional assets. The system uses this label as both punishment and warning: fall outside the norm, and you'll lose access to the very things everyone is told they "need"—credit cards, loans, mortgages, overdrafts, and the perceived safety of a big bank account.

But in the context of true financial liberation, becoming unbankable is about strategic self-exclusion. It means redesigning your life so that you no longer require the toxic products and predatory tools that banks use to control and drain their customers. It's about being so sovereign, self-reliant, and resourceful that the bank loses all power over your money—and, by extension, your life.

Why Banks Want You Bankable (and in Debt)

Banks are not public servants. They are profit machines. Their business model depends on you borrowing money, carrying balances, and paying interest or fees. Every credit product—mortgage, car loan, personal loan, credit card, line of credit—is designed to keep you in a state of managed dependence. Even "free checking" and rewards programs exist to lure you into deeper relationships, encourage more transactions, and upsell debt products.

Your value to a bank is measured not by your savings, but by your borrowing and your fees. As long as you play by their rules—chasing credit scores, maintaining "good standing," and staying perpetually engaged—they win.

But the moment you become financially self-sufficient, the moment you refuse to be a consumer of their core products, you become unprofitable—and, in the best sense, unbankable.

The Steps to Becoming Unbankable (By Choice)

1. Eliminate All Consumer Debt

Debt is the primary tether that banks use to control you. Pay off credit cards, personal loans, car notes, and mortgages as quickly and ruthlessly as possible. The less you owe, the less leverage the bank has.

- Refuse new offers of "pre-approved" credit, no matter how tempting.
- Shred, freeze, or securely store your cards once balances hit zero.
- Don't close accounts right away—simply refuse to use them. Starve the system of your participation.

2. Build and Maintain a Powerful Cash Buffer

Instead of relying on overdraft protection or lines of credit for emergencies, build your own safety net—a robust cash reserve that covers several months of expenses. This empowers you to weather storms, job loss, or medical surprises without crawling to a lender.

- Keep enough in a checking account for easy access, but don't let large sums sit vulnerable to automatic withdrawals, "account maintenance" fees, or institutional risk.
- Consider diversifying where you keep savings—some in reputable credit unions, some in online high-yield accounts, or even in physical cash for true emergencies.

3. Ditch Credit Scores as a Life Goal

The credit score—mythologized as your "financial report card"—is only important if you want to stay in the game of borrowing. For the unbankable, a high score is no longer a badge of honor, but a relic of a system you've left behind.

- If you're not planning to borrow, the score becomes irrelevant.
- Focus on your net worth, not your creditworthiness.
- Let your FICO score fade as you build real, tangible wealth.

4. Master Non-Bank Payment Solutions

Banks want to monopolize your access to money, but you have alternatives. Consider:

- Using credit unions, which are member-owned and less profit-focused.
- Leveraging prepaid debit cards for online purchases, budgeting, or travel.
- Exploring digital wallets and payment apps for person-to-person transactions, especially those that don't tie directly to a major bank.
- When feasible, deal in cash—no fees, no tracking, no exposure to hacks.

5. Break Free from Automatic Dependency

Many people allow banks to run their financial lives automatically—bill pay, direct deposit, autopayments. While convenient, this can make it harder to be truly aware of, and in control over, your money.

- Shift to more active management. Manually pay bills where possible. Review every statement, every month.
- If you have regular income, consider splitting it across multiple institutions to minimize risk and maximize flexibility.

6. Learn to Live Without Bank "Perks"

Banks will dangle perks—points, miles, cashback, overdraft "protection"—to entice you back into their net. Remember, these perks are never free; they are always subsidized by those in debt or by hidden fees.

- Instead of chasing points, ask yourself: does this perk require me to spend more or keep a balance? If yes, it's not a perk—it's bait.
- Enjoy true freedom by choosing experiences, products, and services based on value—not what "rewards" are offered.

7. Embrace Direct and Community-Based Finance

When you need to save, invest, or even borrow for genuine emergencies, seek options outside the traditional banking system:

- Participate in community lending circles, trusted peer-to-peer loans, or family-based financial agreements with clear boundaries.
- Use micro-investing platforms, crowdfunding, or direct investment in businesses or projects you believe in.
- Explore alternative currencies and barter, where appropriate, to meet needs without the bank's involvement.

The Psychological Shift: Reclaiming Financial Sovereignty

Becoming unbankable is more than just moving your money or closing accounts. It's a total shift in mindset—a declaration of independence. You stop seeking validation from institutions designed to profit from your neediness. You become your own underwriter, risk manager, and treasurer.

This self-reliance breeds new confidence. When you are no longer afraid of being rejected by a lender, you're free to make decisions based on your best interests—not the requirements of a loan application or the whims of a faceless algorithm. You stop chasing approval, and start building legacy.

Dealing with Resistance: Myths, Warnings, and the Path Forward

You will face pushback. Friends, family, even financial "experts" may warn you that leaving the system is dangerous, impractical, or even irresponsible. Banks themselves will bombard you with offers and reminders, hoping to lure you back into the fold.

But remember: true financial strength isn't about having the highest credit limit or the shiniest card—it's about having options, resources, and the discipline to say "no" to systems that don't serve you.

The End Game: What It Feels Like to Be Unbankable

Imagine waking up with no payments due, no nervous glances at your credit score, no dread when the bank sends a "special offer." Your emergency fund is yours, unencumbered. Your purchases are deliberate, not dictated by points or perks. You're immune to rate hikes, annual fees, and algorithmic manipulation.

This is the true endgame of Debtburn: not just debt freedom, but *system* freedom. You are no longer a cog in the banking machine. Your wealth, time, and peace of mind belong to you, and you alone.

Conclusion: The Power of Walking Away

Becoming unbankable is the ultimate act of rebellion in a world designed to keep you tethered, tracked, and paying. It is the final stage of financial liberation—when you choose sovereignty over dependence, clarity over confusion, and power over permission.

You won't just survive outside the system—you'll thrive. The banks will label you "unprofitable." You'll know the truth: you're untouchable. And that is freedom no institution can offer—or take away.

Appendix A: Essential Debt Destroyer Tools (Spreadsheets, Apps, Schedules)

Eliminating debt at its root requires more than determination; it demands precision, structure, and the right tools to track, manage, and accelerate your journey. This appendix is your master resource guide—a curated toolkit of analog and digital systems to keep you relentlessly on track, supercharge your strategy, and bring clarity to every dollar. Whether you're a pen-and-paper minimalist or a smartphone power user, these tools are your new allies in the battle for financial liberation.

1. The Debt Inventory Spreadsheet

Your foundational tool for total clarity. A well-built spreadsheet exposes every debt, every due date, and every cent of interest draining your future. Here's how to build it:

A. Core Columns:

- Creditor Name
- Account Number (or Reference)
- Type of Debt (credit card, loan, medical, etc.)
- Total Balance
- Interest Rate (APR)
- Minimum Monthly Payment
- Payment Due Date
- Status (Current, Delinquent, Paid Off)
- Notes (special terms, penalties, contacts)

B. Action Columns (Optional but Powerful):

- Targeted Payoff Date
- Actual Payoff Date
- Snowball/Avalanche Priority Order
- Extra Payment Applied This Month
- Running Balance

C. Templates:

- Google Sheets Debt Snowball Template
- Microsoft Excel Simple Debt Tracker

How to Use:

Update at least once per week. Color code paid-off debts for visual momentum. Review before making any major financial decisions.

2. Budgeting and Payment Scheduling Tools

Controlling cash flow is just as important as tracking balances. The following systems keep you on top of income, expenses, and payment deadlines:

A. Zero-Based Budgeting Spreadsheet

Zero-based budgeting means every dollar has a job—nothing is "left over" or lost to impulse spending. At the start of each month, allocate your income across:

- Fixed Expenses (rent, utilities)
- Minimum Debt Payments
- Extra Debt Payments (target debt)
- Essential Living Costs
- Emergency Savings
- Discretionary/Non-Essential (optional or omitted during a financial fast)

Template Example:

- EveryDollar Zero-Based Budget Spreadsheet
- Google Sheets Zero-Based Budget Template

B. Payment Calendars and Reminders

Missed payments mean fees and lost progress. Set up a simple visual calendar:

- Mark each debt's due date in a paper planner or digital calendar (Google Calendar, iCal).
- Schedule reminders 3 days in advance to allow for transfer delays or emergencies.
- Use recurring tasks on your phone's reminder app or a dedicated habit tracker like Habitica or TickTick.

3. Debt Payoff and Tracking Apps

For those who prefer automation, mobile and web apps can simplify tracking, suggest payoff plans, and visualize your progress. Here are top recommendations:

A. Debt Payoff Apps

- **Undebt.it**
  Free/paid web tool. Input all debts, choose your strategy (snowball, avalanche, custom), and generate a step-by-step payoff plan with charts and milestone projections.
  undebt.it
- **Tally**
  Links your credit cards, recommends payment strategies, and (optionally) automates payments. Good for visual learners who want real-time feedback.
  meettally.com
- **Debt Payoff Planner**
  Mobile app (iOS/Android). Tracks debts, calculates payoff dates, and gives motivation through progress bars and payoff "countdowns."
  debtpayoffplanner.com
- **YNAB (You Need A Budget)**
  Powerful for both budgeting and debt payoff, with proactive tracking, customizable goals, and community support.
  youneedabudget.com

B. General Budgeting Apps (with Debt Features)

- **Mint**
  Free. Links accounts, tracks spending, bills, and debt balances, and sends alerts for unusual activity.
  mint.intuit.com
- **Goodbudget**
  Envelope-based budgeting and debt tracking. Works well for households or shared goals.
  goodbudget.com

4. Payment Acceleration Schedules and Calculators

Crushing debt faster often means making extra payments, but how much difference does that make? These tools show you exactly:

- **Bankrate Debt Payoff Calculator**
  Enter your debts, payment schedule, and any extra amounts to see your payoff timeline and total interest saved.
  bankrate.com/calculators/debt/debt-payoff-calculator.aspx
- **Vertex42 Debt Reduction Calculator**
  Customizable spreadsheet that projects your debt-free date with multiple "what-if" scenarios.
  vertex42.com/ExcelTemplates/debt-reduction-calculator.html
- **NerdWallet Extra Payment Calculator**
  Quick and simple for visualizing how much faster you can get free with extra cash applied monthly.
  nerdwallet.com/article/finance/extra-payment-calculator

5. Printable Progress Trackers and Visual Tools

Tracking your debt-free journey visually can be a powerful motivator. Printable trackers make progress tangible and provide small dopamine hits as you move forward:

- **Debt Thermometer**
  A simple chart you color in as you pay off balances, bringing the "end" closer with each fill.
  Printable Debt Thermometer
- **Milestone Charts**
  Break your debts into smaller goals (e.g., every $500 or $1,000 paid off), and reward yourself (non-monetarily) at each step.
- **Habit and No-Spend Trackers**
  Use habit tracking apps or bullet journal pages to log "no-spend" days, track financial fasts, or reinforce new money habits.
  HabitBull | Bullet Journal Templates

6. Automation and Safeguards

Making your plan "idiot-proof" is critical—especially when life gets hectic.

- **Automatic Transfers:**
  Set up recurring transfers from your main account to a designated debt payment account immediately after each payday.
- **Separate Payment Account:**
  Use a separate checking account solely for debt payments. Transfer your "extra" payment amount each month and set up automatic payments for minimums and targets.
- **Bill Pay Services:**
  Most banks and credit unions offer free bill pay services to automate your payment schedule. Never rely solely on memory!

7. Accountability and Support Tools
The journey is hard—don't go it alone.

- **Online Debt-Free Communities:**
Join groups like Reddit's r/personalfinance, r/debtfree, or YNAB forums for support, advice, and motivation.
- **Accountability Partners:**
Share your plan with a trusted friend or partner. Schedule regular check-ins (weekly or monthly) to celebrate wins and troubleshoot setbacks.
- **Progress Journals:**
Keep a physical or digital diary. Note triggers, triumphs, and lessons learned. Review often to keep yourself grounded and focused.

8. Security and Privacy Considerations
As you deploy digital tools, prioritize your safety:

- Use strong, unique passwords for each financial tool.
- Enable two-factor authentication on all apps and accounts.
- Avoid storing sensitive information in unsecured notes or documents.
- Regularly back up spreadsheets and important files to encrypted cloud storage or an external drive.

Sample Master Debt Destroyer Schedule

Weekly:

- Update spreadsheet/app balances and payments
- Review calendar for upcoming due dates
- Check off "no-spend" days on your tracker

Biweekly:

- Allocate all "extra" income (side gigs, refunds, gifts) to your current debt target
- Revisit your acceleration calculator to check your debt-free ETA

Monthly:

- Reconcile all payments and balances
- Print or update your debt thermometer
- Share your progress with your accountability partner or support group
- Audit your spending habits and adjust next month's budget

Quarterly:

- Review and refine your strategy
- Assess if it's time to switch your payoff target or adjust the plan for changing circumstances
- Celebrate progress—plan a non-financial reward

Final Note: Customize and Iterate

No two journeys to debt freedom are identical. Mix, match, and adapt these tools to your personality and lifestyle. The only requirement is action—consistent, focused, and relentless.

With these tools in hand, you hold the keys to the control room of your financial life. Your old debts no longer have the upper hand. The numbers are clear, the strategy is set, and victory is just a matter of time and persistence.

Light the fire. Track every dollar. Obliterate every balance. This is your Debt Destroyer Arsenal—wield it without mercy.

Appendix B: 90-Day Total Reset Challenge

The journey to obliterate debt isn't a series of scattered efforts—it's a sustained campaign. The "90-Day Total Reset Challenge" is your war plan: a structured, transformative regimen that attacks debt, rewires your money habits, and recalibrates your mindset for lasting financial freedom. This is not a soft "try your best" experiment; it's a firebrand commitment to break old cycles, ignite new momentum, and prove—once and for all—that you can rewrite your financial destiny.

Challenge Overview

Over the next 90 days, you will:

- Conduct a total financial inventory and deep self-assessment
- Deploy targeted "debt torpedo" tactics for fast payoff
- Embark on a period of financial fasting to break spending addictions
- Aggressively raise your income and slash expenses
- Build an emergency buffer and pivot away from bank dependency
- Cement new money habits through daily, weekly, and monthly rituals
- Track and celebrate every milestone with fierce accountability

Each phase builds on the last. By the end, you won't just be closer to debt freedom—you'll be fundamentally transformed.

Preparation: Before You Begin

- **Print or Save This Appendix.** Keep it visible.
- **Pick a Start Date.** Don't delay—momentum is everything.
- **Recruit an Accountability Partner or Join a Community.** You'll go further with support.
- **Set Up Your Debt Destroyer Toolkit.** (See Appendix A)
- **Get a Journal, Planner, or Digital Notes App.** Daily reflection is required.

The Three Phases

Phase 1 (Days 1–30): Total Clarity & First Strike

Objective: Strip away confusion, face your debts, and fire your first torpedo.

Key Actions:

1. **Complete a Full Financial Inventory**
    - List every debt (balance, interest, minimum payment, due date).
    - List all regular income sources.
    - List all monthly expenses (fixed and variable).
2. **Choose Your "Target Debt"**
    - Select either the smallest debt (for quick win) or highest-interest debt (for maximum savings).
    - Organize remaining debts by payoff order.
3. **Build a Zero-Based Budget**
    - Allocate every dollar. Assign extra funds to your target debt.
4. **Launch Financial Fasting**
    - For 30 days, spend only on essentials (food, housing, utilities, medicine, transport).
    - Track every cent. Note triggers, cravings, and wins in your journal.
5. **Automate or Schedule All Debt Payments**
    - Never miss a payment. Set up reminders/automation (see Appendix A).
6. **Visualize Your Progress**
    - Create a debt thermometer, payoff chart, or digital tracker.
7. **Daily Ritual:**
    - Review your debts and budget each morning or night.
    - Write a 3-sentence journal entry on your mindset and spending triggers.

End-of-Phase Goal:

Destroy your first "target debt" or make significant progress. Feel the momentum.

Phase 2 (Days 31–60): Income Surge & Lifestyle Detox

Objective: Accelerate payoff with new money and deeper spending cuts.

Key Actions:

1. **Identify and Launch One New Income Stream**
    - Overtime, freelance, gig work, selling unused items, or digital side hustle.
    - Funnel 100% of extra earnings into your target debt.
2. **Intensify Your Financial Fast**
    - Cut or pause subscriptions, cancel non-essential services, find free alternatives.
    - Keep cash spending for absolute needs only.
3. **Optimize Essentials**
    - Renegotiate bills, switch providers, meal prep to save on food, carpool or use public transport.
4. **Track All "Found Money"**
    - Tax refunds, rebates, cash gifts, sales proceeds—apply directly to debt.
5. **Weekly Ritual:**
    - Update your debt inventory and payoff chart.
    - Reflect on your journal: What patterns do you notice? What small victories have you had?

End-of-Phase Goal:

See a dramatic drop in at least one major debt. Build a $500–$1,000 emergency buffer if possible.

Phase 3 (Days 61–90): System Exit & New Foundations

Objective: Finish strong by fortifying your position and breaking free from old systems.

Key Actions:

1. **Break Bank Dependency**
    - Shift to credit unions, prepaid cards, or digital wallets where possible.
    - Build systems for manual, conscious money management.
2. **Review Credit Products**
    - Shred or freeze credit cards with zero balances.
    - Remove saved card numbers from online stores and apps.
3. **Build Resilience**
    - Continue financial fasting, with a "no-spend" weekend or full week.
    - Increase your emergency fund if possible.
4. **Set up Post-Challenge Habits**
    - Weekly: Update debts and spending.
    - Monthly: Review goals, budget, and savings.
    - Quarterly: Reassess your income ceiling, seek growth opportunities.
5. **Celebrate Milestones**
    - For every debt paid off, celebrate with a non-monetary reward.
    - Share your progress with your accountability partner or community.

Final Ritual:

- Write a letter to yourself about how far you've come, the habits you've changed, and the future you claim from here.

Daily and Weekly Schedules
Daily:

- Check budget/spending log
- Journal for 3–5 minutes (mindset, triggers, small wins)
- Mark progress on debt tracker

Weekly:

- Review all debt balances
- Update budget and adjust plan
- Accountability check-in (partner, friend, group)

Monthly:

- Reassess income and expenses
- Update emergency fund total
- Set new short-term and long-term goals

Troubleshooting & Resilience Tips

- **If you slip, don't quit.** Reset immediately—progress, not perfection.
- **If emergencies arise, use your buffer, not new debt.** Rebuild the buffer next.
- **If motivation flags, revisit your journal and celebrate small wins.**
- **If resistance from others arises, remind yourself: this challenge is for *your* future.**

Victory Checklist

- All debts inventoried and tracked
- At least one debt torpedoed (paid off)
- Financial fast completed (with slip-ups tracked and learned from)
- New income stream created
- Emergency buffer established
- Credit products deactivated/removed
- New systems for budgeting, payment, and savings installed
- 90 days of journals, tracking, and progress recorded
- A sense of control, hope, and momentum restored

Your Reset, Your Revolution

The next 90 days will not always be easy—but the discomfort is temporary, and the transformation is permanent. The 90-Day Total Reset Challenge is your crucible: a test of discipline, courage, and vision. Finish strong, and you'll emerge not just with less debt, but with a new identity—one who chooses freedom over fear, and power over passivity. This is your financial revolution. Burn the old scripts. Write your new future.

The clock starts now. Are you ready?

Message from the Author:

I hope you enjoyed this book, I love astrology and knew there was not a book such as this out on the shelf. I love metaphysical items as well. Please check out my other books:

-Life of Government Benefits

-My life of Hell

-My life with Hydrocephalus

-Red Sky

-World Domination:Woman's rule

-World Domination:Woman's Rule 2: The War

-Life and Banishment of Apophis: book 1

-The Kidney Friendly Diet

-The Ultimate Hemp Cookbook

-Creating a Dispensary(legally)

-Cleanliness throughout life: the importance of showering from childhood to adulthood.

-Strong Roots: The Risks of Overcoddling children

-Hemp Horoscopes: Cosmic Insights and Earthly Healing

- Celestial Hemp Navigating the Zodiac: Through the Green Cosmos

-Astrological Hemp: Aligning The Stars with Earth's Ancient Herb

-The Astrological Guide to Hemp: Stars, Signs, and Sacred Leaves

-Green Growth: Innovative Marketing Strategies for your Hemp Products and Dispensary

-Cosmic Cannabis

-Astrological Munchies

-Henry The Hemp

-Zodiacal Roots: The Astrological Soul Of Hemp

- **Green Constellations: Intersection of Hemp and Zodiac**

-Hemp in The Houses: An astrological Adventure Through The Cannabis Galaxy

-Galactic Ganja Guide

Heavenly Hemp
Zodiac Leaves
Doctor Who Astrology
Cannastrology
Stellar Satvias and Cosmic Indicas
Celestial Cannabis: A Zodiac Journey
AstroHerbology: The Sky and The Soil: Volume 1
AstroHerbology:Celestial Cannabis:Volume 2
Cosmic Cannabis Cultivation
The Starry Guide to Herbal Harmony: Volume 1
The Starry Guide to Herbal Harmony: Cannabis Universe: Volume 2
Yugioh Astrology: Astrological Guide to Deck, Duels and more
Nightmare Mansion: Echoes of The Abyss
Nightmare Mansion 2: Legacy of Shadows
Nightmare Mansion 3: Shadows of the Forgotten
Nightmare Mansion 4: Echoes of the Damned
The Life and Banishment of Apophis: Book 2
Nightmare Mansion: Halls of Despair
Healing with Herb: Cannabis and Hydrocephalus
Planetary Pot: Aligning with Astrological Herbs: Volume 1
Fast Track to Freedom: 30 Days to Financial Independence Using AI, Assets, and Agile Hustles
Cosmic Hemp Pathways
How to Become Financially Free in 30 Days: 10,000 Paths to Prosperity
Zodiacal Herbage: Astrological Insights: Volume 1
Nightmare Mansion: Whispers in the Walls
The Daleks Invade Atlantis
Henry the hemp and Hydrocephalus

10X The Kidney Friendly Diet
Cannabis Universe: Adult coloring book

Hemp Astrology: The Healing Power of the Stars

Zodiacal Herbage: Astrological Insights: Cannabis Universe: Volume 2

Planetary Pot: Aligning with Astrological Herbs: Cannabis Universes: Volume 2

Doctor Who Meets the Replicators and SG-1: The Ultimate Battle for Survival

Nightmare Mansion: Curse of the Blood Moon

The Celestial Stoner: A Guide to the Zodiac

Cosmic Pleasures: Sex Toy Astrology for Every Sign

Hydrocephalus Astrology: Navigating the Stars and Healing Waters

Lapis and the Mischievous Chocolate Bar

Celestial Positions: Sexual Astrology for Every Sign

Apophis's Shadow Work Journal: **:** A Journey of Self-Discovery and Healing

Kinky Cosmos: Sexual Kink Astrology for Every Sign

Digital Cosmos: The Astrological Digimon Compendium

Stellar Seeds: The Cosmic Guide to Growing with Astrology

Apophis's Daily Gratitude Journal

Cat Astrology: Feline Mysteries of the Cosmos

The Cosmic Kama Sutra: An Astrological Guide to Sexual Positions

Unleash Your Potential: A Guided Journal Powered by AI Insights

Whispers of the Enchanted Grove

Cosmic Pleasures: An Astrological Guide to Sexual Kinks

369, 12 Manifestation Journal

Whisper of the nocturne journal(blank journal for writing or drawing)

The Boogey Book
Locked In Reflection: A Chastity Journey Through Locktober
Generating Wealth Quickly:How to Generate $100,000 in 24 Hours
Star Magic: Harness the Power of the Universe
The Flatulence Chronicles: A Fart Journal for Self-Discovery
The Doctor and The Death Moth
Seize the Day: A Personal Seizure Tracking Journal
The Ultimate Boogeyman Safari: A Journey into the Boogie World and Beyond
Whispers of Samhain: 1,000 Spells of Love, Luck, and Lunar Magic: Samhain Spell Book
Apophis's guides:Witch's Spellbook Crafting Guide for Halloween
Frost & Flame: The Enchanted Yule Grimoire of 1000 Winter Spells
The Ultimate Boogey Goo Guide & Spooky Activities for Halloween Fun
Harmony of the Scales: A Libra's Spellcraft for Balance and Beauty
The Enchanted Advent: 36 Days of Christmas Wonders

Nightmare Mansion: The Labyrinth of Screams
Harvest of Enchantment: 1,000 Spells of Gratitude, Love, and Fortune for Thanksgiving
The Boogey Chronicles: A Journal of Nightly Encounters and Shadowy Secrets
The 12 Days of Financial Freedom: A Step-by-Step Christmas Countdown to Transform Your Finances
Sigil of the Eternal Spiral Blank Journal
A Christmas Feast: Timeless Recipes for Every Meal
Holiday Stress-Free Solutions: A Survival Guide to Thriving During the Festive Season
Yu-Gi-Oh! Holiday Gifting Mastery: The Ultimate Guide for Fans and Newcomers Alike

Holiday Harmony: A Hydrocephalus Survival Guide for the Festive Season

Celestial Craft: The Witch's Almanac for 2025 – A Cosmic Guide to Manifestations, Moons, and Mystical Events

Doctor Who: The Toymaker's Winter Wonderland

Tulsa King Unveiled: A Thrilling Guide to Stallone's Mafia Masterpiece

Pendulum Craft: A Complete Guide to Crafting and Using Personalized Divination Tools

Nightmare Mansion: Santa's Eternal Eve

Starlight Noel: A Cosmic Journey through Christmas Mysteries

The Dark Architect: Unlocking the Blueprint of Existence

Surviving the Embrace: The Ultimate Guide to Encounters with The Hugging Molly

The Enchanted Codex: Secrets of the Craft for Witches, Wiccans, and Pagans

Harvest of Gratitude: A Complete Thanksgiving Guide

Yuletide Essentials: A Complete Guide to an Authentic and Magical Christmas

Celestial Smokes: A Cosmic Guide to Cigars and Astrology

Living in Balance: A Comprehensive Survival Guide to Thriving with Diabetes Insipidus

Cosmic Symbiosis: The Venom Zodiac Chronicles

The Cursed Paw of Ambition

Cosmic Symbiosis: The Astrological Venom Journal

Celestial Wonders Unfold: A Stargazer's Guide to the Cosmos (2024-2029)

The Ultimate Black Friday Prepper's Guide: Mastering Shopping Strategies and Savings

Cosmic Sales: The Astrological Guide to Black Friday Shopping

Legends of the Corn Mother and Other Harvest Myths

Whispers of the Harvest: The Corn Mother's Journal

The Evergreen Spellbook

The Doctor Meets the Boogeyman

The White Witch of Rose Hall's SpellBook

The Gingerbread Golem's Shadow: A Study in Sweet Darkness

The Gingerbread Golem Codex: An Academic Exploration of Sweet Myths

The Gingerbread Golem Grimoire: Sweet Magicks and Spells for the Festive Witch

The Curse of the Gingerbread Golem

10-minute Christmas Crafts for kids

Christmas Crisis Solutions: The Ultimate Last-Minute Survival Guide

Gingerbread Golem Recipes: Holiday Treats with a Magical Twist

The Infinite Key: Unlocking Mystical Secrets of the Ages

Enchanted Yule: A Wiccan and Pagan Guide to a Magical and Memorable Season

Dinosaurs of Power: Unlocking Ancient Magick

Astro-Dinos: The Cosmic Guide to Prehistoric Wisdom

Gallifrey's Yule Logs: A Festive Doctor Who Cookbook

The Dino Grimoire: Secrets of Prehistoric Magick

The Gift They Never Knew They Needed

The Gingerbread Golem's Culinary Alchemy: Enchanting Recipes for a Sweetly Dark Feast

A Time Lord Christmas: Holiday Adventures with the Doctor

Krampusproofing Your Home: Defensive Strategies for Yule

Silent Frights: A Collection of Christmas Creepypastas to Chill Your Bones

Santa Raptor's Jolly Carnage: A Dino-Claus Christmas Tale

Prehistoric Palettes: A Dino Wicca Coloring Journey

The Christmas Wishkeeper Chronicles

The Starlight Sleigh: A Holiday Journey

Elf Secrets: The True Magic of the North Pole

Candy Cane Conjurations

Cooking with Kids: Recipes Under 20 Minutes

Doctor Who: The TARDIS Confiscation

The Anxiety First Aid Kit: Quick Tools to Calm Your Mind

Frosty Whispers: A Winter's Tale

The Infinite Key: Unlocking the Secrets to Prosperity, Resilience, and Purpose

The Grasping Void: Why You'll Regret This Purchase

Astrology for Busy Bees: Star Signs Simplified

The Instant Focus Formula: Cut Through the Noise

The Secret Language of Colors: Unlocking the Emotional Codes

Sacred Fossil Chronicles: Blank Journal

The Christmas Cottage Miracle

Feeding Frenzy: Graboid-Inspired Recipes

Manifest in Minutes: The Quick Law of Attraction Guide

The Symbiote Chronicles: Doctor Who's Venomous Journey

Think Tiny, Grow Big: The Minimalist Mindset

The Energy Key: Unlocking Limitless Motivation

New Year, New Magic: Manifesting Your Best Year Yet

Unstoppable You: Mastering Confidence in Minutes

Infinite Energy: The Secret to Never Feeling Drained

Lightning Focus: Mastering the Art of Productivity in a Distracted World

Saturnalia Manifestation Magick: A Guide to Unlocking Abundance During the Solstice

Graboids and Garland: The Ultimate Tremors-Themed Christmas Guide

12 Nights of Holiday Magic

The Power of Pause: 60-Second Mindfulness Practices

The Quick Reset: How to Reclaim Your Life After Burnout

The Shadow Eater: A Tale of Despair and Survival

The Micro-Mastery Method: Transform Your Skills in Just Minutes a Day

Reclaiming Time: How to Live More by Doing Less

Chronovore: The Eternal Nexus

The Mind Reset: Unlocking Your Inner Peace in a Chaotic World
Confidence Code: Building Unshakable Self-Belief
Baby the Vampire Terrier
Baby the Vampire Terrier's Christmas Adventure
Celestial Streams: The Content Creator's Astrology Manual
The Wealth Whisperer: Unlocking Abundance with Everyday Actions
The Energy Equation: Maximize Your Output Without Burning Out
The Happiness Algorithm: Science-Backed Steps to Joyful Living
Stress-Free Success: Achieving Goals Without Anxiety
Mindful Wealth: The New Blueprint for Financial Freedom
The Festive Flavors of New Year: A Culinary Celebration
The Master's Gambit: Keys of Eternal Power
Shadowed Secrets: Groundhog Day Mysteries
Beneath the Burrow: Lessons from the Groundhog
Spring's Whispers: The Groundhog's Prediction
The Limitless Mindset: Unlock Your Untapped Potential
The Focus Funnel: How to Cut Through Chaos and Get Results
Bold Moves: Building Courage to Live on Your Terms
The Daily Shift: Simple Practices for Lasting Transformation
The Quarter-Life Reset: Thriving in Your 20s and 30s
The Art of Shadowplay: Building Your Own Personal Myth
The Eternal Loop: Finding Purpose in Repetition
Burrowing Wisdom: Life Lessons from the Groundhog
Shadow Work: A Groundhog Day Perspective
Love in Bloom: 5-Minute Romantic Gestures
The Shadowspell Codex: Secrets of Forbidden Magick
The Burnout Cure: Finding Balance in a Busy World
The Groundhog Prophecy: Unlocking Seasonal Secrets
Nog Tales: The Spirited History of Eggnog
Six More Weeks: Embracing Seasonal Transitions
The Lumivian Chronicles: Fragments of the Fifth Dimension

Money on Your Mind: A Beginner's Guide to Wealth
The Focus Fix: Breaking Through Distraction
January's Spirit Keepers: Mystical Protectors of the Cold
Creativity Unchained: Unlocking Your Wildest Ideas in 2025
Manifestation Mastery: 365 Days to Rewrite Your Reality
The Groundhog's Mirror: Reflecting on Change
The Weeping Angels' Christmas Curse
Burrowed in Time: A Groundhog Day Journey
Heartbeats: Poems to Share with Your Valentine
Dino Wicca: The Sacred Grimoire of Prehistoric Magick
Courage of the Pride: Finding Your Inner Roar
The Lion's Leap: Bold Moves for Big Results
Healthy Hustle: Achieving Without Overworking
Practical Manifesting: Turning Dreams into Reality in 2025
Jurassic Pharaohs: Unlocking the Magick of Ancient Egypt and Dino Wicca
The Happiness Equation: Small Changes for Big Joy
The Confidence Compass: Finding Your Inner Strength
Whispers in the Hollow: Tales of the Forgotten Beasts
Echoes from the Hollow: The Return of Forgotten Beasts
The Hollow Ascendant: The Rise of the Forgotten Beasts
The Relationship Reset: Building Better Connections
Mastering the Morning: How to Win the Day Before 8 AM
The Shadow's Dance: Groundhog Day Symbolism
Cupid's Kitchen: Quick Valentine's Day Recipes
Valentine's Day on a Budget: Love Without Breaking the Bank
Astrocraft: Aligning the Stars in the World of Minecraft
Forecasting Life: Groundhog Day Reflections
Bleeding Hearts: Twisted Tales of Valentine's Terror
Herbal Smoke Revolution: The Ultimate Guide to Nature's Cigarette Alternative
Winter's Wrath: The Complete Survival Blueprint for Extreme Freezes.

The Groundhog's Shadow: A Tale of Seasons
Burrowed Insights: Wisdom from the Groundhog
Sensual Strings: The Art of Erotic Bondage
Whispered Flames: Unlocking the Power of Fire Play
Forgotten Shadows: A Guide to Cryptids Lost to Time
Six Weeks of Secrets: Groundhog Day's Hidden Messages
Shadows and Cycles: Groundhog Day Reflections
The Art of Love Letters: Crafting the Perfect Message
Romantic Getaways at Home: Turning Your Space into Paradise
Purrfect Brews: A Cat Lover's Guide to Coffee and Companionship
The Groundhog's Wisdom: Timeless Lessons for Modern Life
The Shadow Oracle: Groundhog Day as a Predictor
Emerging from the Burrow: A Journey of Renewal
The Language of Love: Learning Your Partner's Love Style
Authorpreneur: The Ultimate Blueprint for Writing, Publishing, and Thriving as an Author
Weathering the Seasons: Groundhog Day Perspectives
Valentine's Day Magic: A Guide to Romantic Rituals
The Shadow Chronicles: Stories of Groundhog Day
Love and Laughter: Fun Games for Valentine's Day
AstroRealty: Unlocking the Stars for Property Success
The Groundhog's Path: A Guide to Seasonal Balance
Groundhog Day Diaries: Reflections in the Shadow
The Groundhog's Light: Illuminating the Path Ahead
Valentine's Traditions from Around the World
AI Wealth Revolution: Unlocking the Trillionaire Mindset
Love Rekindled: Reigniting Passion in Relationships
Single and Thriving: Self-Love on Valentine's Day
Emerald Legends: Mystical Tales of Ireland
Green Alchemy: Harnessing Nature's Magic
The Hearts of Horror: A Valentine's Day Nightmare

The Leprechaun's Guide to Wealth and Wisdom

Dancing with the Sidhe: Celebrating the Otherworld

Shamrocks and Shadows: Mysteries of the Green Isle

Emerald Energy: Harnessing Luck and Growth

The Gingerbread Golem's Valentine: A Sweetheart's Guide to Love and Enchantment

The Celtic Knot: Weaving Life and Destiny

Green Fire: Elemental Magic for St. Patrick's Day

Clover Chronicles: Finding Your Inner Luck

Ireland's Mystical Creatures: A Field Guide

Gingerbread Golem's Love Almanac

Prowl and Thrive: The Lion's Guide to Success

Love Alchemy: Transforming Your Life Through Heart Energy

WORLD DOMINATION: Woman's Rule 3:The New Life

The Midnight Rose: A Guide to Lunar Love Spells

The Forbidden Letters: Writing Your Own Love Prophecy

Luck and Lore: St. Patrick's Day for Modern Mystics

The Green Path: A Pagan Celebration of Renewal

The Dark Architect's Guide to Reprogramming Reality

Prankster's Paradise: A Guide to Harmless Hijinks

Manifest Your Reality: The Law of Attraction Simplified

The TARDIS Owner's Manual: Understanding the Doctor's Ship: *A complete guide to the TARDIS, its technology, secrets, and mysteries*

Starlit Romance: Astrology Secrets for Finding True Love

The Time Lord's Atlas: A Complete Guide to the Whoniverse: ***A breakdown of the locations, planets, and dimensions explored in Doctor Who***

Sweetheart Shadows: The Dark Side of Love and Attraction

February Fire: Reigniting Passion in Every Area of Life

The Self-Love Toolkit: 5 Ways to Embrace Who You Are

February Sparks: Ignite Your Dreams in 28 Days

March to Success: A 31-Day Action Blueprint
Ancient Paths: The 13 Sacred Principles of Dino Wicca
Echoes of Tomorrow: Navigating the AI Revolution
The Wellness Blueprint: Balancing Mind, Body, and Soul
Green Horizons: Sustainable Living for a Better Tomorrow
The AI Wealth Code: How to Make Millions with Automation
AI-Powered Creativity: Writing, Art, and Music for Profit
Extinction Rites: Rebirthing Your Soul Through Prehistoric Magick
Sacred Serpents tarot
Celestial Enchantment blank journal
Star Strains
Culinary Journeys: Exploring Global Flavors at Home
The Hollowvale Curse
The Hollowvale Harvest
The Egg of Transformation: Awakening Your Inner Power
Blooming Into Power: A Wiccan Guide to Spring Awakening
The Nightmare Nexus: The Third Doctor's Perilous Haunting
Digital Detox: Reclaiming Your Life in a Connected World
Ostara's Path: Walking the Spiral of Renewal
The Sacred Hare
Financial Freedom: Building Wealth in the Modern Age
Spring's Cauldron: Stirring the Waters of Change
The Hollowvale Pact
Quantum Consciousness: The Science of Reality Shifting
The Hollowvale Hunger
The Sacred Waters Within: A Witch's Guide to Hydrocephalus Magick
The Raven's Nest: Building a Life of Unshakable Stability
AI and the Human Mind: The Future of Intelligence
The Hollowvale Reckoning
Timeless Love: Building and Maintaining Lasting Relationships

The Raven's Roar: Unlocking Unstoppable Confidence
Raven Sight: Awakening Intuition and Inner Wisdom
The Butterfly Effect: Small Changes, Big Transformations
Taming the Boogeyman: How to Conquer Your Inner Fears
The Magick of Green: Awakening Earth's Energy in You
The Entrepreneurial Mindset: Secrets to Business Success
The Hollowvale End
The Shadow Luck Ritual: Reclaiming Power from Your Dark Side
Spring Magick for Beginners: A Simple Guide to Seasonal Energy Work
Doctor Who: The Hollowvale Conundrum
The March of Miracles: Unlocking Synchronicities in Spring
Unveiling the Cosmos: A Guide to Stargazing and Space Exploration
The Ultimate Guide to Surviving an Economic Collapse
The AI Gold Rush: How to Profit from the AI Revolution
Bastet's Shadow: The Hidden Power of Feline Magick
The Bastet Codex: Unlocking the Goddess's Magickal Secrets
Purring Spells: Harnessing Bastet's Healing Frequencies
Bastet's Nine Lives: Rebirth, Transformation, and Immortality Spells
Primal Currents: Hydrocephalus Magick in the Path of Dino Wicca
The Digital Gold Rush: Mastering E-Commerce and Online Sales
Future Shock: Adapting to the Next Decade of Change
The Quantum Mindset: Think Like a Billionaire
Sacred Motherhood: Awakening the Divine Feminine Within
The Mother's Spellbook: Enchantments for Love, Protection, and Prosperity
The Witch's Guide to Parenting: Raising Empowered and Intuitive Children

The Magick of Motherhood: Reclaiming Your Power Through Rituals

The Pagan Path to Self-Love: A Goddess's Guide to Worth and Confidence

Wild Woman Magick: Unleashing Your Primal Power

The Money Magnet Blueprint: Unlocking Unlimited Wealth

Biohacking 101: Unlock Your Body's Full Potential

The Wild Father: A Pagan Guide to Strength and Wisdom

The Sacred Masculine: Unlocking Your Inner Power

The Druid's Compass

The Warrior's Mindset

The Father's Fire

Odin's Path

Ancestral Bonds

The House That Whispers

The Magician's Code

The Wild Hunt

The Green Man's Path

The Altar of Success

The Shadow and the Sword

The High Priestess's Guide to Energy Healing

The Lunar Mother

The Sacred Self-Care Grimoire

The Womb Wisdom Codex

The Wheel of the Mother

The Witch's Guide to Manifestation

The Q2 Reset

The Ultimate Guide to AI-Powered Passive Income

Escape the 9-5

AI Feline Fortunes

The Tear-Stained Grimoire

Razorblade Runes

Cemetery Sirens

The Midnight Wristwatch
The Town That Forgets
AI Horror & Creepypasta
The Hollow Frequency
The Breach Echo
The Quiet Between Worlds
The Sigil of Tharan-Khul
Summon the Vault of Y'ha'ten
The Becoming Codex
The Profit of Az'ra-nar
The Drowned Logos
Echoes of the Eldritch Will
The Deep Ledger
Necronomicon of Networth
Covenant of the Wealthwyrm
The Whisperer's Manifesto
The Rites of Azh-K'luth
The Ark of the Crawling Coin
The Tithe of Shadows
Inkheart Abyss
The Timewinds of Y'ha-nthlei
The Spiral Labyrinth of Azag-Nirrh
The Gallifreyan Heresy of the Black Pharaoh
The Psalms of Nyog-Sotha
Black Rain Alchemy
The Infinite Maw
The Entropic Blueprint
The Oracle of Sh'guul
The Book of Breach
The Drowned Saint's Testament
Dreamcraft of the Sleeper God
The Silence Market
Cthonomics: The Dark Wealth Algorithm

Invocation of the Ten-Eyed King
Wealthbound to the Wyrm Below
Become the Unnameable
Codex of the Sovereign Flame
Rituals of Relentless Becoming
The Shadow Ascends
The Eyes Beneath You
The Will That Wakes Worlds
Silence Is a Weapon
The Mirror That Screams
The Whisper Between Moments
The Mind That Devours Fear
The Myth of the Finished Self
The Architect of Your Madness
The Voice You've Buried
The Discipline of Madness
Stormborn: Awakening Your Inner Tempest
The Mind That Ate Time
Unbind Your Becoming
The Pact You Owe Yourself
The Devourer's Diet
The Acid That Carves the Path
The Tower You Must Burn
The Breath Between Worlds
Speak Like the Deep
The Labyrinth Within
The Spine of the Sea God
Rejection Is a Portal
The Crown You Refused
The Scar Is the Spell
The Lightless Flame
The Habit of Becoming Horrific
ChickenJockey Chaos

The Gatekeeper Within
You Are Not Your Name
The Compass of the Mad
The Archive of Unsent Letters
What the Mirror Can't Show You
The Knife You Needed
Worship Nothing, Become Everything
The Other Voice
The Body the World Forgot
The Vein of the Void
The Black Bone Codex
The Puzzle of the Hidden Self (Millennium Puzzle)
The Eye That Sees the Lie *(Millennium Eye)*
The Ring of Return (Millennium Ring)
The Rod of Relentless Will ***(Millennium Rod)***
The Tally of the Soul (Millennium Tauk/Necklace)
The Key to the Locked Timeline (Millennium Key)
The Scale of Sacred Decisions (Millennium Scales)
Inferno Bites: The UnOfficial Minecraft Lava Cookbook
Rot in the Attic
Prana: The Hidden Force of Your Infinite Self
The Shadow Realm Within: Transforming Darkness Into Destiny
The Borderland Collapse
Claws of Protection: Bastet's Defensive Magick
Mr. Ring-a-Ding's Madness
Yugioh Astrology: Celestial Deckcraft and Duel Destiny (2026–2027 Edition)
The Seal You Signed: Unlocking the Power You Once Feared
The Puzzle of Infinite Minds: Unlocking the Mentalism Hidden Within
The Eye That Mirrors the All: Secrets of Inner Reflection
Doctor Who: The Toymaker's Broadcast

Rootwake: The Carbon Covenant
Skitter Logic: Unlearning the Fear That Built You
Doctor Who: The World That Froths
Rootwake: The Fizz That Rewrites Flesh
Rootwake: Frothfather of the World
The Holly Pact: Blood Beneath the Mistletoe
The 2nd Mass Principle: Building Unbreakable Tribes
Web of Wits: A Survival Guide to Encounters with Anasi the Spider (Aunt Nancy)
The Hexbreaking Handbook: Effective Spells to Remove Curses
Pop Alchemy: Transform Your Life One Sip at a Time
The Mason Code: Leading in Unleadable Times
Petosiris and the Fifth Chamber of Thoth
The Ether Seed Within
The Parent of Tomorrow
Petosiris's Pyramid of Perpetual Wealth
Unlearn the World
Grimoire of the Hollow Tongue
Zodiac Weeds: Finding Your Strain Through the Stars
Aquarius Rises in the Bank
The Sugar God's Smile
The Skinclock Reversal: Biohacking the Face of Time

Get Some Tarot cards: https://www.makeplayingcards.com/sell/apophis-occult-shop

Get some shirts: https://www.bonfire.com/store/apophis-shirt-emporium/

<u>Instagrams:</u>
@apophis_enterprises,
@apophisbookemporium,
@apophisscardshop
Twitter: @apophisenterpr1
Tiktok:@apophisenterprise
Youtube: @sg1fan23477
Hive: @sg1fan23477
CheeLee: @SG1fan23477

Podcast: Apophis Chat Zone: https://open.spotify.com/show/5zXbrCLEV2xzCp8ybrfHsk?si=fb4d4fdbdce44dec

Newsletter: https://apophiss-newsletter-27c897.beehiiv.com/

If you want to support me or see posts of other projects that I have come over to: **buymeacoffee.com/mpetchinskg**

I post there daily several times a day

Get your Dinowicca or Christmas themed digital products, especially Santa Raptor songs and other musics. Here: **https://sg1fan23477.gumroad.com**

Apophis Yuletide Digital has not only digital Christmas items, but it will have all things with Dinowicca as well as other Digital products.

www.ingramcontent.com/pod-product-compliance
Lightning Source LLC
LaVergne TN
LVHW022023200926
848481LV00007B/2509
* 9 7 9 8 3 4 9 3 8 7 4 1 8 *